Oh

An ode to old loves
Not feeling the same
How strange the changes came
Sad to see an end
Taking beyond a friend

All the many secrets
Spilled like spirit egrets

Weren't we so natural
our nervous laughs
And oh, the many secrets
Still spilling from the past

With my regrets and grief
Hope you'll keep this
Part of me in peace
Not to lay awake and wish to be
More away less sorry

Lost in memories
Save the best of me in you
And sleep gently in truth
Who knows what we'd do
Given the chance to change
thrown away each day

Silence Seed

What and what
The grit in this cut
Tucked between
A seamless sucker theme

Is it me
All unprepared
Split the scene
But I'm just scared

You might use me
Find amusing
All these things

Creases in the skin
Fake feeling settles in
Cracks the plaster
Pours out of a mold
Too suited for disaster

On and on
I am told
This one's not my hand
How and when to fold

With eyes almost shut to wonder
What silence pulses thunder
From fingertips slight and quick

Unbutton one then unzip

Reveal all the tables flipped
one furious storm behind
A fire quenched by wine
Where still the ashes stain
Bruised for miles
And whose choice to cause such pain

Might have been both
Who smiles quickly wane
How distant they remain

Some steamy fog covers
Which monster is named

Old lovers wronged
Another blame they lay
Where roses grow
Let the sun come up
Let it rain

Let old lovers love
Or softly curse my name

For the attention

Calling out to hear the sound

More than to feel eyes on me
How the ground may want me found

Wanting

Swallowed up in stone
Write a theory about fear
In tears so all alone
Just like I said I always wanted to be
Don't remember if I believed
But if you want to come home
haunt it
and I swear I'll never leave

So am I all hung out to dry
With tears left to cry

What a shame
You don't need an alibi
Don't need to change

Just listen for the other side
Experiential claim
To lay unsatisfied
Waiting for the day
We realize our mistakes

It's not you I need to change
But you I hope to see
I tell myself every day

To show you my belief

How I'd hope to be viewed
And give the same in return
If no other truth shines through
God how this one burned

*

I'm not aloof
I'm afraid
And I've learned
Not to betray
From the taste of betrayal
ways in which we all might fail

How the weight lands
The bruises slow to fade
I weight my own hands
With steady progress made

In the wind

Current state
Pulled aloft
Along
Apart

Re-assimilating too slowly

Some small things escape

Dust motes hidden notes
Swing and sway
On a windless day

A winding chorus
Calls up a tightening path
Lips soft fingers hard
Lightning shocks do ask

If I feel it too
The chaos and madness
Of being pulled into you

Blown apart in art
Rendered whole in truth
For all you'd push aside
Feeling caught in a loop
I know this lie
And can't abide
All I'm due

Do we protect a dream from being
Or reality from seeming

*

A great mystery rests on your tongue
Say the truth
May we not come undone
And have what is issued

A strong bond
a gentle soul
Perhaps too fond
Not to exact a toll

For the folly of lovers
And the binding tie of love

Pleasures supple treasures
And broken bits of trust

Less like the vines they grew into
But glass in the dust
From things I threw at you
Before I even knew myself
Boy, I knew you too well

What is all wrong

Standing in the doorway
Same spot where I told you to leave

Feels like I'm wasting away
Don't want to believe
I've made a big mistake
No one hears me plead

No one's here
And I need
Need to think
It was the right thing

Can't stand what I can't change
And if it wasn't my thing
Why didn't the feeling go away
When you left

And why did my heart break
Empty out my chest

Alone as I said I would be
Failed in a way
To know a good thing

Escape in sleep
wake tired of everything I've done

my nightmare legs can't run
fire the sun
let the night be at one
with my quiet love

Just lay still and stare
Reflection's like a drug
Scattered prism rainbows
in sunbeams full of dust

*

in a mood lingering
Far too sad
To not be grief

A loss suspended
In old disbelief
Running from wounds
I swore were healed

Before you I was subsumed
our scars each revealed

The holes in our armor
Matched from disparate wars
Made it so much harder
When it crashed in our doors
And dragged us both away
Into a pain yet paid

Tried for other crimes
to say no it isn't mine
and make it yours

then wish you'd come back

try to make it more
than a flash in a fire
we didn't put out
rather retire what remains in doubt

it wasn't you who made my mistakes or my pain
truth is they seem to fade away
the longer you remain

it makes me uncomfortable to know you

you see the distant smoke
you see where I am injured
where my heart once broke
I am trusting you to trace with gentle fingers
All the breaks and fissures

Hoping you know
How not to hurt me
Odd how the thought alone
Seems a lot like fighting dirty

Were I better at seduction
I'd just trust you to be yourself
Adjust to the feeling of subduction
let these things be well

if I knew the answer I'd ask the question

but in ignorance don't dare
hesitate, make broad suggestions
afraid of how much I care

*

all the ways I feel exposed
least of these my wondering
if you could possibly feel the thundering
doubts in my head

they reach my mouth
breach what I won't let myself say
reach the place
where I'd hope you'd want to stay

sabotage is an inside job
from a one woman show
I paid a lot for what I've been taught
Which is surely more than I know

I hold on to you in this way
Your truth in mine

It’s not the mistake
But the passage of time
It’s a current a currency
Respect and dignity

I see your strength
And grow for the sight
You know you’ll be alright
Disparate futures, separate lives
Or the kind which aligns over time

I will see you in light more than shadow
And use the influences well
Better than if I had known
We’d drag ourselves through hell

*

I might be tired but it’s not a flaw
The fight and the fire
Back’s against the wall

Seemingly asleep
Tender heart safe to keep

Should you need reassuring
Your company doesn’t disturb me

Better in time silence preferring
To soak into the clay
Rest beside me and stay

To sculpt the dust and ash
Half empty or full
Both remain the same glass

*

The trenches I've dug deep
The rut
The cut
Round little knees
I'd cry
These scrapes sear
But why
Who would hear

Deep in the woods
Off in the cut
Up to no good
Let them tell you what
I've done
If not how I've grown
Stuck in my rut
Who would have known
"If you hadn't come
Maybe I'd go"

I say it, that lie
Then lay very still
Under a changing sky

Running
somehow paralyzed
At the same time
from a fear I've never truly felt
And one I don't understand
ringing ears a weighted belt
Heavy backside hand

Why won't you change
They seem to say
Don't even know if I can

Some part of me wrestles with ease
Taking it down below

What grew from discord?
A forest, of course
Perhaps all I'll ever have to show
One long war
Deep rut
Tall trees
a long steep road home
skinned knees
strangely satisfying

*

Without the threat of death

What is life

A never ending paradise
Never ending need
An end, unseemly thing
Seems worth a look
Worthwhile to try and see

How profound a moment
Seconds to the last
Every torment stolen
Perhaps again to ask
Did I do well
Here, where I have made myself?

*

Each breath precious and deep
If I didn't know
That I don't know
Perhaps I'd just sleep

But the breaths come fast

Steeped in mysteries
Temporary each

I am collecting within these things
Just out of reach
One among scattering beliefs

Caught in the breach
Suspended in love
To learn, to teach
To be one among

More surely as time goes by
It is right to live
Until it's time to die
time punctuates the same page
same lines
words my own, but not only mine

Gifts from everyone I've heard
loves I've never known
written words like stones thrown
Glad now for the crowd
Much as time spent alone

It's not forever
we are here for a time
That's the treasure
That we are here we're alive

*

How we tried
Sublime guilty sighs and signs
It's been time
It's been time

Familiar as your smell

The times you wished me well
How hard we both fell
To fall apart

Lost in art and darkness
The world fails to start
Let's rest our wings
Under the eaves

Remembering I believed
We'd never need another thing

You'd never leave
Another beginning
seems
Empty to me

Trying too hard to get your attention
Resenting not knowing what to say
For all I failed to mention
Each time you'd go away
I felt it break
Tried to imagine the same
Inside you
Felt it breaking every day
Just like I do
Just the same

Get out the bottle
Drink these worries off
Searing hot to swallow
It's the tears that make me cough

I won't tell you that
Might say pride
is all I have
But I don't like to lie
And I didn't want it back

After all it's done
I am at one with love and loss
Collateral damage in between
The fighter and a cause
Both armies were me
And every soldier now dying
A heart and mind divided
Over which one is lying
Oh it was all me the whole time
This broken heart is mine
And it's no trophy
It's a scar
Found my honor where we are
Here and now

It's a lie, you follow
Say the words so soft
I don't want to cry these tears
And make it real

But it's all alive inside
The loss is all I feel

Maybe tomorrow
Today will be great
My own willful sorrow
Caught on much too late

To stop myself
From pushing you too far

Here I did not do well
In this place where I broke your heart

Trying to keep mine intact
I broke that too
And it's all I have
Would give it right to you

Just to take back what I've done
To know peace, to show you
I do truly know love

it was you the whole time
I was out of my mind from the fear of it
Heart so reduced pained even to hear of it

Those days were wasted in pretend
I'd take any bit of it
and reclaim my friend
Who has been hurt by a fight
He didn't provoke
Words unsaid
Because no one spoke

And I lacking sight
From a wounded spirits smoke
No magic imbued
words I wish could be removed
drove the light from my room

I wish I'd never believed
things I hoped you wouldn't do
but couldn't show you

I could hold on more peacefully
Just to know for a moment
You saw the good in me
When I couldn't see yours

Not too much to ask
perhaps so much more
than too much to ask
I surrender the floor
It is yours

Wish you'd occupy it still
Be free to receive
Free to remain of your will

I wanted that unbelievably
disbelief deceived me

Now a lesson turned in the dirt
This fragile piece of me
Has grown and I have learned
In such a hard way

To carry disgrace gracefully
It takes a certain weight off me
Missing you so deeply as I do

Carry the meaning and the truth
And if it aches to see you change
I need to feel it and let it be

To make my own way
In healing find peace

*

The defenseless closing doors
Leveraging satisfaction
Resentment

Proliferation in pain
Ashamed thinking you don't see me
Don't want to see these
Welts internally swelling

A desire rising
To be assured
I made the word
You finally heard

The silence to spawn
Maybe a firm handed reaction
Oh to be sure we've carried on
You know the moves

A dance a shoe
Stepping on toes
Not so inured
As to ignore the war
Which matters more
to you

Why can't I see returned
These offerings lightly spurned

Something good in me
In your eyes, please

Stark scenes down low
Outside our view
But I think you know
How we become what we do

So I in hope will wait
To divine the truth about you in me
not easily replaced
we are in the ether
and you are everything

this life tied
to the one I've yet to live

the spark a drive
seems I need to forgive

all of us better
this fine frail tether

pulls notes from my throat
and tears from my eyes

you have been a dream to me
it's time I realize
when to open my eyes

the time which tells
the tears that fall

I've come to this well
To slake a thirst for it all

Where I fell
May again yet fall

Got our tale left to tell
No part of it too small

I'll take the meaning take the mess
Take whatever's left

long as you remain
I will ever speak your name

With a kindness and hope
From the heart you nearly broke

Still beating in this chest
Reeling from the test

It hasn't taken out the best of me to die
It felt like a beating
Just the feeling was a lie

*

The best of me comes into being
Every single time
I'm at the end
My soul begins again

Hanging by the thinnest thread

Every word I've said
Tried by the same
To rise instead
of being weighted by
a time spent in vain

my love, as one
my love calls out to you
to forgive and overcome
all I can't undo

I wished I could be
a bit better than I was
at accepting the reality
and receiving real love

it's just so new
didn't know what to do
to flourish
doesn't grow overnight
too discouraged to surrender
but not too weak to fight
fragile but not tender
not in any way alright

if I hadn't noticed I'd let you down
this cold abyss would hold me
until I finally drowned

this broken heart saved me
though it also betrayed me

offering this one thing if you'll let me
I'm proud of you, now
and hope you never forget me

Branded in Scars

Drag that broken leash to me

I'd set you free and keep you anyhow

Minding things falling down around us

If I never had found love

I'd never have known

One thing to call me home

sleeping longer than I need

For rest

It's a test to breathe

In this atmosphere

So choked with lost souls

Carbon and tar

Having exacted a toll

I didn't make it far

Before the memory of you
Woke me up to then pursue
The same dreams as I had when was sleeping
But where the sun can touch my face

No longer in nightmares weeping
Falling from deep space
Back in time, it is time

I was missing all those days
They weren't wasted
And I'm not sorry
Tell old loves all the same

Not to worry
No lost greatness
These connections remain

Different directions
But the location stays the same

Making changes
all that I will claim
From our time spent together
respects your true name
Keeping real a treasure
Who we both became

Our truth purified by fire
I am not the same
Neither of us a liar
Taking different truths away

I'll learn more tomorrow
From things you said yesterday
Only the time was borrowed
Love in this soul comes to stay

No matter where or if ever again
Memories unfair, scorn or pretend

It isn't abrupt finality
Everything didn't end
But to adjust to reality
each of these wheels spins again

Some more slowly

Barely touching

Things we can't defend

The brace of all our shames

Collected in themes

made all these mistakes

To understand what that means

And what we take away

You educated me

No need to retaliate

Though I felt it in the foment

Tired of stormy moments

Snared by the neck and kicking

sounds in my mouth foaming

hissing and clicking

Without eyes to see

Lashing out untrue to me

What could I do to you
No better thing
than I knew
at the time

The broken-hearted mind
Is no lover
But needing the same
I'd yet to discover
How cruel the pain
can be

From one to another
Lost in deceit
The same thing I did to you
I did to me, and it hurt me, too

It's where I learned and how I fell
How it burned dragged us through hell
Not knowing how to show
All I didn't ever know
But now I do
Thanks to you
All we put each other through

The purpose to define

What of life becomes divine

In a better light

We did just fine

Swine and Glory

Years go by faster and faster

Doomed to cry

The tears of a bastard

A cost he will not pay

To drag some broken piece away

And hear the laughter

He refuses truth

all he won't say

I'll not demand from you

Don't need apologies anyway
Not some disconnected youth
Caught in the fray
But knowing what I do
Will come to stay
And I might come unglued
when my guilt
Is as correct as innocence

I can bring a soul to you
Not unchanged but in balance
For all the pain I've been through
Glad for the challenge

It's a vivid mind
And these thoughts align
Inflexibility fades
A brittle quality
Like paint chips away

Never quite followed a path
Often forgot to stop and ask where I am
Not lost or knowing the lay of the land
Reading misplaced stakes

From the back of a fan
Cooling my face

Waiting for grace
To understand
If I should simply stay like a trace
Or make a plan
Ever in the way
Losing sight of land
By myself betrayed
Before the same judge I stand

Ready to change
While remaining who I am

The tricky part
Trying not to ruin
My own healing heart
Not knowing what I'm doing

Captivated by the way
water moves

The grace of a mean
With nothing to do
Except to be

A breach in between these worlds
Some nights such a fight
Mind in a whirl
Stomach full of butterflies
Hand too tightly curled

As I watch other girls go by
And wonder if I'm at all like them
Or maybe they pretend to be alright
Some fragile nature to defend
With their heads up higher
than mine has ever been

Feel so different in my own eyes
Sliding with the shadows
In the fog around the lamplight
As you look outside your window
Do you feel it stirring inside you?
What I would give to know
A soul in whole and truth

And to be able to show
I have one too
even afraid
I'm glad I came
glad I stayed
even to have found some so untrue
they broke away a heavy weight
while I floated up to you
tied themselves to hate and fell
a crucible went through such hell
and came out a gentle flame
close as I came to that gate
finding the fire to save myself
I found in kind
feeling brave is the same
as waiting until later to cry
might be pitiful, a shame
just to be alive
but I'll feel it every day
and sleep quite well at night
owning the way I came
and all the times I was not right
complex to explain
pale in direct light

a ghost by some other name

just trying to assimilate

minding that in time

this is the self I will face

and can I stand the sight?

Squint and look again

Wandering through ruins

Trusses diagonal collapse

Feeling nearly human

Circumstantial perhaps

These hands are moving

Mind shifts to recycle

The disfigured cripple inside assuming

I'll never need this smile

But it's pressed in the clay

Blown about by a stillness

Waiting out the day
Restless unfulfillment

Strategically placed
Saying, “hey, can you feel this?”

Because I do
I do

Can’t prove out the lie
You know, and you knew

Didn’t you feel me cry
If I ever were untrue

You’d know it deep inside
Gone as the last day

Quiet as the one to follow
All the words I couldn’t say

Now make it hard to swallow

Places his hands have been

There are no words
Just our ghosts
Haunting each others skin

the one I feel the most
When I wonder where he is

Free to move without
The roiling doubt within

So afraid to want
My soul hides below

Each memory a leaf blown from this tree
The life inside aching to see
A truth too divine not to push aside the lies

Drunk on a fire
Burning off my time

It’s such desire

Within to reside

Without to reveal

How tender and fine

This skin can truly feel

Sought to be returned

A lifetime taught and learned again

The light of this life

Resonance without end

Love is a presence to never pretend

And I am dying in this

Not sure how to defend

The very thing I wish to give away

Afraid of being hurt again

More afraid of being afraid

To Make a Fairy Tale

A debaser and one so deceived
Race against each other
In ways make themselves believe

They are right to take flight
Eyes averted from the light making them blind
And I on ascent feeling my own mind
thinking madness in my head

Hands raw from a grip holding back death
Blood left behind from the trail to the ledge
Upward ever slowly
each breath like blame
nerves edge electric flame
prickling a needle tipped with pain

Working to survive only loss to gain
The life inside me beating ever away
It hurt when no one came

When they laughed in my face
For trying to escape our valley

From the damp and darkness made

The sunlight atop the ridge always called me
So I went, and it might have been the wrong thing

Sometimes I just wish for a bed to sleep in
Remembering food I've eaten

The ones from above
Calling down also have no love
They come to the edge to curse my name

Those running in reverse
Playing the same game
But in their special way
Taking more risk
None greater than this
To pressure a divide
of these follies mine
seems to be the least

Just the granite, chalk and lime
And burrs beneath my skin
I'd go back down but this time

My pride is too deeply dug in

Not wanting to hear or even see
The people who sneer and laugh at me
Displaced in a way, and now physically
In between
Unwilling to say

I can't follow a dream
To live in the light of day
Because those around me
Don't believe in such a thing

I keep climbing and trying
But never really seem
To get very far
The others above yell down to give up
It doesn't leave a mark
Just tiny ache in a heart

With ears too tired to listen
Can't feel the friction
Tension they try to stoke
They're not in my position

Plenty of breath to provoke

they call down insults for a while
to make each other smile
imagining how powerfully
the stones they throw hurt me
but they usually miss
one blows a mocking kiss
and everyone seems proud
of their places on the ground

From somewhere high above
I hear a cry and look up
To see bodies falling legs splayed
Hear screams halting
Less hateful, more afraid
No longer calling insults
Their voices beg for a result
Impossible

I feel the cold fear like a shock wave
Hear more truth in those seconds
Four among a group
So low they had collected

Stones to weigh them down
Dented in the ground
In pools black and unreflective
At one with the mud and dust
In the dark
Where there was an 'us'

And I too far to go back now
It weighs on my heart
As a crowd gathers round
The dead and dying strangers
Whose words claimed a familiarity
False as an accusation endangered
And received
The wrong thing believed
Impunity, not immunity
Ones own force not to be ignored
While presence is a lesson
A game, even with no score
Ends poor for grand critics
Seeking fodder to treat as meat

Crumpled on the ground
at their perceived inferiors feet

Come down, come down

Stricken family in the valley yell up at me

And I will not

There's no helping the dead

And I still am caught

The thought in my head

I've got to, I've got

To live in the light

Not the stone cold darkness

Keeping me awake at night

The echoes clipped of water and cliffs

Bouncing all the hollow sounds

Rumbles of thunderous rocks falling down

I have to go

It's all I know

Beyond the crippling doubt

That I'm already gone

And won't ever belong

In the light or darkness beside

This worry aches my heart

Dust and tears sting my eyes

I know I'm right

Though it feels wrong

Will myself to go on

Even if I die tonight

In the exact same place

In the very same way

I've paid too high a price

The desire far too great

I allow for just one minute

For my soul to settle in this

The very fact I'm trying

Makes life worth dying to have

Not knowing if I'll get there

I am here

It's this fact

that pushes me to move

to plan and act

it's this fact, itself to prove

my honor's bled into these stones

what may lay ahead

I carry my home to the unknown

The fight is in me
It's why I don't let go
Join these offering to be enemies
when I'd rather be alone
Than make my life a mockery
Broken down below
Even if it happens
It's not why I have this
Pressure inside to climb until I die

Each one may believe this thing
Others are wrong thus enemies
to destroy
Of me, too, who can know
But that energy's no toy
It drives the body
Steals the soul
Leaves a heartbeat dry
And a body cold

Lived a life but to die
For nothing but an impression
Perhaps that's my lesson
Pulling out a truth

I don't move my hands for you

To make an impression

Hold your tongue

When your guesses all reveal

Your own soul and mind

How you might feel

What fire drives another to despise

To terrify or humiliate

Try to change a mind

or way not their own

It's a consideration for a lonely fate

No trust for being known

Perhaps a life seeming wasted

To those above and below

Such an affront to these

Whose miseries

Collect until they flow

All the pebbles and words they hurled at me

How quickly these things go

From searing cruel memories

To sorrow, and to hope

Fleeting energies

In the vacancies grow

While I scrape my knees

On a dangerous precipice with no rope

No hold

Flashes of disaster in my mind

For not doing what I'm told

There are those I've loved in life

Who'd gladly see me fall

I missed them most of all

When they stood before me

vanishing

carried with the echo of their words

trying to force me to a crawl

disbelieving, felt and heard

no loft at the summit

not a reason to stall

but to overcome

it's no difference at all

when the alternative

and inevitable

are at one with gravity

the wind drives straight down

to the madness in me

and I can't help but love it

for dragging out my fire

no cheering crowd

no time to retire

from below or above

this triumph is mine

sublime, alone in love

alive

if ever unknown

inside

that doubt sleeps with dead memories

keeps getting into things

subdued by the passage of time

just like I am,

mine

and I'm not changing

without reason to fear
those humiliating sneering faces

should others speak critically
some day see clearly
and hear
their own voice
the sear, the choice
to reach with feeble fingers
into ears of spirits
they will feel and also hear it
in time come to fear it
as they break inside themselves
casting others into their hell
without the power
to span that gap
pretend to tower
over those who have
witnessed the fools
and their destruction
hand thrown tools of instruction
down in the blood they lost
their souls also cost

with their lives

out like a light they'd try to hide

in ringing distortion

the truth crackling back in

no ridicule or force

could make me shed this skin

for a flawless veneer

drive those voices back in

let them weep

push their intentions reflected deep

I do not want them, they're yours to keep

Get away with nothing

As you are to me

And I to you

deflection

Spoken forcefully

Without a spark of truth

My flaws are steady here

Their claws have shredded tears

From my eyes

Took my smile for a time

carrying out such theater

the stale dread of shame
making fun seems a meager feast
how they make a name
off stolen letters
and passed off regrets
for the smug numbness
of forsaking oneness
for a fracture manufactured
to please a group of useless fools
will make a shame of you

their time was won
in their minds at least
it seemed like fun
to be a beast
to believe cruelty is strength
and I paid a piece
for these misbegotten beliefs
no worries
paid in bloody fists
to see what's beyond a ridge
I may never reach
Fine lesson
to teach myself

while I pulse and fade
those who came to hate my name
their own pulse to claim

this direction's mine to take
this soul is owed to change
it's a gift to be we say
so chosen to make my way
it can't be blocked by hate
by spiteful wills and talk
of how I seem
we meet the breach and break
toward our own infinity

maybe they didn't know
again I know I don't
though I stand unwilling
to let the brittle hand of man
displace me
nor do their actions disgrace me

if they learned in their lesson

the object did display

my end can be the same

best to stay out of the way

let each wear down their trail

instead of working to make them fail

wish me well or horrible stories to tell

let mercy replace what I hate of myself

I'll not listen to the tale

Of how I seem

for having less to say

I have heard the screams

At the end of the game

Not much mystery

A spirit faked

Breaks more easily

they never recognized grace

before their moment passed

I didn't laugh

when they died on their backs

Having my own death to face

Rather figure out how

To get back up

While so much pulls me down

Not needing to look away

Right now

gravity is the hound at my heels

Let love resound

How you might feel it too

That is your own

Let yourself be known

Perhaps I'll see you

At the top, on the ledge

Perhaps I'll come along and stop

And ask you what you said

When my face was pressed to the boulders

Might find silence is truly best

The spirit you test

Will offer you no rest

Let it be your own

making peace with your best

grow in the light
or climb up from the dark

don't forget to put aside
just how small you are

yesterday
how others may seem
they, like tomorrow
like being lost in a dream

wake where you are
knowing you'll go far

and if you don't stop
to throw rocks at strangers

it's really not that dangerous
to just be yourself

the love, the pity
how alone we've all felt

better lies to romanticize
gazing up into the sky

glad to be alive for this time
don't want to chase the moments away
trying to make them stay
or seem more glorious
than being here today

it's good right now
I make it good now
Nothing else I'd rather be
Ashes, water and dust
And the energy between

Printed in Great Britain
by Amazon

71929168R00033